March 2012

FINANCIAL AUDIT

American Battle Monuments Commission's Financial Statements for Fiscal Years 2011 and 2010

Highlights of GAO-12-404, a report to congressional committees

FINANCIAL AUDIT

American Battle Monuments Commission's Financial Statements for Fiscal Years 2011 and 2010

Why GAO Did This Study

Created in 1923, the American Battle Monuments Commission (the Commission) operates and maintains 24 American military cemeteries on foreign soil; 25 federal memorials, monuments, and markers; and 7 nonfederal memorials. For fiscal year 2011, the Commission incurred program costs of $71.5 million to maintain its cemeteries and federal memorials.

In accordance with 36 U.S.C. § 2103, GAO is responsible for conducting audits of the agencywide financial statements of the Commission. GAO audited the financial statements of the Commission for the fiscal years ended September 30, 2011, and 2010.

The audits were done to determine whether, in all material respects, (1) the Commission's financial statements were presented fairly and (2) Commission management maintained effective internal control over financial reporting. GAO also tested the Commission's compliance with selected laws and regulations.

What GAO Recommends

GAO is not making any recommendations in this report, but will be reporting separately on matters identified during its audit, along with recommendations for strengthening the Commission's internal controls.

In commenting via e-mail on a draft of this report, the Commission concurred with GAO's findings and conclusions.

View GAO-12-404. For more information, contact Steven J. Sebastian at (202) 512-3406 or sebastians@gao.gov.

What GAO Found

In GAO's opinion, the financial statements of the American Battle Monuments Commission (the Commission) as of September 30, 2011, and 2010, and for the fiscal years then ended, are presented fairly, in all material respects, in conformity with U.S. generally accepted accounting principles (GAAP). Also, in GAO's opinion, although certain internal controls over financial reporting should be improved, the Commission maintained effective internal control over financial reporting as of September 30, 2011. In addition, GAO found no reportable instances of noncompliance with the laws and regulations it tested.

GAO found a significant deficiency in the Commission's internal control over financial reporting as of September 30, 2011. Specifically, GAO identified vulnerabilities in access controls over the payroll systems that maintain and process foreign employee payroll. In addition, GAO found that the Commission did not have clear policies and procedures outlining the specific duties and responsibilities of its Human Resources and Finance Directorates for processing of foreign employee payroll. These deficiencies increase the risk of undetected errors or irregularities in processing the Commission's foreign payroll. GAO also found that the Commission took action to provide an analysis of the agency's overall financial position and results of operations in its fiscal year 2011 Management's Discussion and Analysis as required by U.S. GAAP and Office of Management and Budget Circular No. A-136, *Financial Reporting Requirements*.

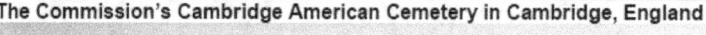

The Commission's Cambridge American Cemetery in Cambridge, England

Source: American Battle Monuments Commission.

_____ United States Government Accountability Office

Contents

Abbreviations

ABMC	American Battle Monuments Commission (the Commission)
FMFIA	Federal Managers' Financial Integrity Act of 1982
MD&A	Management's Discussion and Analysis
OMB	Office of Management and Budget

United States Government Accountability Office
Washington, D.C. 20548

March 1, 2012

The Honorable Patty Murray
Chairman
The Honorable Richard Burr
Ranking Member
Committee on Veterans' Affairs
United States Senate

The Honorable Jeff Miller
Chairman
The Honorable Bob Filner
Ranking Member
Committee on Veterans' Affairs
House of Representatives

In accordance with 36 U.S.C. § 2103, this report presents the results of our audits of the financial statements of the American Battle Monuments Commission (the Commission) for the fiscal years ended September 30, 2011, and 2010. This report contains our (1) unqualified opinion on the Commission's fiscal years 2011 and 2010 financial statements; (2) opinion that the Commission maintained, in all material respects, effective internal control over financial reporting as of September 30, 2011; and (3) conclusion that our tests of the Commission's compliance with selected provisions of laws and regulations for fiscal year 2011 disclosed no instances of reportable noncompliance during fiscal year 2011. The accompanying report also provides information regarding a significant deficiency we identified concerning the Commission's internal control over financial reporting related to its payroll processes for foreign employees.

We are sending copies of this report to other interested congressional committees. We are also sending copies to the Acting Director of the Office of Management and Budget, the Commissioners and Secretary of the Commission, and other interested parties. In addition, the report is available at no charge on the GAO website at http://www.gao.gov.

Should you or your staff have any questions concerning this report, please contact me at (202) 512-3406 or at sebastians@gao.gov. Contact points for our Offices of Congressional Relations and Public Affairs may be found on the last page of this report.

Steven J. Sebastian
Managing Director
Financial Management and Assurance

United States Government Accountability Office
Washington, D.C. 20548

To the Commissioners and Secretary of the American Battle Monuments Commission

In accordance with 36 U.S.C. § 2103, we are responsible for conducting audits of the agencywide financial statements of the American Battle Monuments Commission (the Commission). In our audits of the Commission's financial statements for fiscal years 2011 and 2010, we found

- the consolidating financial statements as of and for the fiscal year ended September 30, 2011, and comparative consolidated totals as of and for the fiscal year ended September 30, 2010, are presented fairly, in all material respects, in conformity with U.S. generally accepted accounting principles;

- although certain internal controls should be improved, the Commission had effective internal control over financial reporting as of September 30, 2011; and

- no reportable noncompliance with the selected provisions of laws and regulations we tested.

The following sections discuss in more detail (1) our basis for these conclusions; (2) our conclusions on the Commission's Management's Discussion and Analysis and other supplementary information; (3) our audit objectives, scope, and methodology; and (4) Commission comments.

Opinion on Financial Statements

The Commission's consolidating balance sheet as of September 30, 2011, consolidating statement of net cost and changes in net position, and consolidating statement of budgetary resources, with accompanying notes for the fiscal year then ended, and comparative consolidated totals as of and for the fiscal year ended September 30, 2010, are presented fairly, in all material respects, in conformity with U.S. generally accepted accounting principles.

Opinion on Internal Control

Although certain controls should be improved, as discussed below, the Commission maintained, in all material respects, effective internal control over financial reporting as of September 30, 2011. Commission internal control provided reasonable assurance that misstatements, losses, or noncompliance material in relation to the consolidating financial statements would be prevented or detected and corrected on a timely basis. Our opinion is based upon criteria established under 31 U.S.C. § 3512 (c), (d), commonly known as the Federal Managers' Financial Integrity Act of 1982 (FMFIA).

Significant Deficiency

During fiscal year 2011, we identified several deficiencies in the Commission's internal controls over its payroll processes for its non-U.S. citizen employees (foreign employees).[1] These deficiencies include vulnerabilities in access controls over the Commission's payroll systems for its foreign employees and weaknesses in its policies and procedures over payroll processing for foreign employees. While these deficiencies, individually and collectively, do not constitute a material weakness in internal control over financial reporting,[2] they nevertheless increase the risk of undetected errors or irregularities in the processing of the Commission's foreign payroll and, ultimately, in the Commission's financial statements. Consequently, we believe they collectively represent a significant deficiency in the Commission's internal control.[3]

To fulfill its mission, the Commission employs both U.S. citizens and foreign employees. U.S. citizens are considered federal employees, while foreign employees are hired pursuant to treaty agreements and respective foreign national employment law. Payroll for all of the Commission's federal employees is managed by the General Services Administration and these employees are paid using electronic funds transfers from the U.S. Department of the Treasury (Treasury). Payroll for the foreign

---

[1] During fiscal year 2011, the Commission used a total of 396 full-time equivalent positions. U.S. citizens constituted 73 positions, while the remaining 323 positions were non-U.S. citizens employed at the Commission's regional offices and at the cemeteries in the countries where the Commission operates.

[2] A material weakness is a deficiency, or combination of deficiencies, in internal control over financial reporting, such that there is a reasonable possibility that a material misstatement of the entity's financial statements will not be prevented, or detected and corrected on a timely basis. A deficiency in internal control exists when the design or operation of a control does not allow management or employees, in the normal course of performing their assigned functions, to prevent, or detect and correct misstatements on a timely basis.

[3] A significant deficiency is a deficiency, or a combination of deficiencies, in internal control that is less severe than a material weakness, yet important enough to merit the attention of those charged with governance.

employees, which covers employees located in seven countries, is maintained by the Commission in three separate payroll systems.[4] Foreign employees enter their time and attendance for each pay period into their respective country's payroll system. Time charges at the end of each pay period are reviewed and certified by designated accountants in the Commission's Finance Directorate. The payroll systems then calculate the payroll and generate reports detailing each foreign employee's gross and net pay, including offsetting deductions and other benefits and allowances. Once these reports are verified and certified as to reasonableness by the designated accountants, the payroll systems generate payroll files that are sent to both Treasury for the disbursement of employee wages and to the Commission's financial management system for recording in the general ledger.

During our audit, we identified deficiencies in controls over the three foreign employee payroll systems that increased the risk of financial reporting misstatements and unauthorized access and manipulation of the systems or their data. Specifically, we found that two system administrators had inappropriate system access allowing them to not only make system changes but to alter data in systems for which they were responsible. These administrators were responsible for (1) developing, (2) testing, and (3) implementing the foreign payroll systems and any changes to them, which included the systems used to process their own payroll. With this level of access, these administrators had inappropriate authority to alter data in the payroll systems and modify the payroll files sent to Treasury for payroll disbursement and to the general ledger for recording. Such actions could enable the administrators to add or alter system data without authorization and not have any such changes readily detectable by Commission management. We also found that the Commission had not installed critical updates on several of its servers, leaving these servers vulnerable to unauthorized users who could gain full administrator-level access through a server that communicates with the Internet. This, in turn, could allow unauthorized users to gain administrator-level access to the foreign employee payroll systems.

In addition to the deficiencies in controls over access to the foreign payroll systems, we found that the Commission did not have effective controls to

---

[4] The Commission maintains payroll for foreign employees located in the following countries: (1) Belgium, (2) England, (3) France, (4) Italy, (5) Luxembourg, (6) the Netherlands, and (7) Tunisia.

minimize the risk of errors in processing of payroll actions for the Commission's foreign employees. Specifically, we found that the Commission did not have policies and procedures clearly delineating the responsibilities of both the Human Resources and Finance Directorates with respect to ensuring accurate payroll information for foreign employees. While the Human Resources Directorate is responsible for processing all employee personnel actions, such as promotions, salary increases, and benefit changes, the Commission did not have procedures that set out required steps to be followed to transmit employee actions processed by the Human Resources Directorate to the Finance Directorate. Because the Finance Directorate is responsible for verifying and approving employee information in the payroll systems, including the certification of time charges and salary and benefits information, the lack of such sufficiently detailed procedures increases the risk of undetected errors in reporting payroll information. As a result of these deficiencies, during our testing of foreign payroll, we identified instances in which the information in the foreign employee payroll systems was out of date and annual leave hours were incorrectly recorded.

While these deficiencies increased the risk of errors and misstatements in foreign employee payroll amounts occurring and not being timely detected and corrected, the Commission also had certain budgetary controls in place that would have detected and corrected any material misstatements in a timely manner. Consequently, we do not believe these control deficiencies constitute a material weakness in the Commission's internal control over financial reporting. However, we do believe that these deficiencies, collectively, represent a significant deficiency in internal control that merits attention by those charged with governance.

We also identified other less significant matters concerning the Commission's internal control that we will report separately, along with recommended corrective actions for these matters as well as for the matters comprising the significant deficiency in internal control.

Compliance with Laws and Regulations

Our tests of the Commission's compliance with selected provisions of laws and regulations for fiscal year 2011 disclosed no instances of noncompliance that would be reportable under U.S. generally accepted government auditing standards. However, the objective of our audit was not to provide an opinion on overall compliance with laws and regulations. Accordingly, we do not express such an opinion.

Consistency of Other Information

The Commission's Management's Discussion and Analysis (MD&A) and other information related to heritage assets presented in the Commission's financial report contain a wide range of data, some of which are not directly related to the financial statements. We do not express an opinion on this information. However, we compared this information for consistency with the financial statements and discussed the methods of measurement and presentation with officials of the Commission. On the basis of this limited work, we found no material inconsistencies with the financial statements, U.S. generally accepted accounting principles, and Office of Management and Budget (OMB) Circular No. A-136, *Financial Reporting Requirements*.

During our audit of the Commission's fiscal year 2010 financial statements,[5] we determined that the Commission did not provide an analysis of the agency's overall financial position and results of operations in its MD&A as required by U.S. generally accepted accounting principles and OMB Circular No. A-136. However, as part of our fiscal year 2011 financial audit, we found the Commission's fiscal year 2011 MD&A included such an analysis in accordance with U.S. generally accepted accounting principles and OMB Circular No. A-136.

Objectives, Scope, and Methodology

Commission management is responsible for (1) preparing the financial statements in conformity with U.S. generally accepted accounting principles, (2) establishing and maintaining effective internal control over financial reporting and evaluating its effectiveness, and (3) complying with applicable laws and regulations. Commission management evaluated the effectiveness of its internal control over financial reporting as of September 30, 2011, based upon the criteria established under FMFIA. Commission management's assertion based on its evaluation is included in appendix I.

We are responsible for planning and performing the audit to obtain reasonable assurance and provide our opinion on whether (1) the Commission's financial statements are presented fairly, in all material respects, in conformity with U.S. generally accepted accounting principles and (2) Commission management maintained, in all material respects,

---

[5] GAO, *Financial Audit: American Battle Monuments Commission's Financial Statements for Fiscal Years 2010 and 2009*, GAO-11-320 (Washington, D.C.: Mar. 1, 2011).

effective internal control over financial reporting as of September 30, 2011. We are also responsible for (1) testing compliance with selected provisions of laws and regulations that have a direct and material effect on the financial statements and (2) performing limited procedures with respect to certain other information accompanying the financial statements. In order to fulfill these responsibilities, we

- examined, on a test basis, evidence supporting the amounts and disclosures in the financial statements, including evidence supporting statistical samples of Commission payroll and nonpayroll expenditures;[6]

- assessed the accounting principles used and significant estimates made by Commission management;

- evaluated the overall presentation of the Commission's financial statements;

- obtained an understanding of the Commission and its operations, including its internal control over financial reporting;

- considered the Commission's process for evaluating and reporting on internal control over financial reporting based on criteria established under FMFIA;

- assessed the risk of (1) material misstatement in the Commission's financial statements and (2) material weakness in its internal control over financial reporting;

- tested relevant internal control over the Commission's financial reporting;

- evaluated the design and operating effectiveness of the Commission's internal control over financial reporting based on the assessed risk; and

---

[6] These statistical samples were selected primarily to determine the validity of activities reported in the Commission's financial statements. We projected any errors in dollar amount to the population of transactions from which they were selected. In testing some of these samples, certain attributes were identified that indicated deficiencies in the design or operation of internal control. These attributes, where applicable, were statistically projected to the appropriate populations.

- tested compliance with selected provisions of the following laws and regulations: the Commission's enabling legislation codified in 36 U.S.C. Chapter 21; public laws applicable to the World War II Memorial Fund; Buffalo Soldiers Commemoration Act of 2005; Continuing Appropriations Resolution, 2010; Consolidated Appropriations Act, 2010; Continuing Appropriations Act, 2011; Full-Year Continuing Appropriations Act, 2011; Antideficiency Act; Pay and Allowance System for Civilian Employees; and Prompt Payment Act.

An entity's internal control over financial reporting is a process affected by those charged with governance, management, and other personnel, the objectives of which are to provide reasonable assurance that (1) transactions are properly recorded, processed, and summarized to permit the preparation of financial statements in conformity with U.S. generally accepted accounting principles, and assets are safeguarded against loss from unauthorized acquisition, use, or disposition and (2) transactions are executed in accordance with the laws governing the use of budget authority and other laws and regulations that could have a direct and material effect on the financial statements.

We did not evaluate all internal control relevant to operating objectives as broadly established under FMFIA, such as controls relevant to preparing statistical reports and ensuring efficient operations. We limited our internal control testing to testing controls over financial reporting. Our internal control testing was for the purpose of expressing an opinion on the effectiveness of internal control over financial reporting and may not be sufficient for other purposes. Consequently, our audit may not identify all deficiencies in internal control over financial reporting that are less severe than a material weakness. Because of inherent limitations in internal control, internal control may not prevent or detect and correct misstatements due to error or fraud, losses, or noncompliance. We also caution that projecting any evaluation of effectiveness to future periods is subject to the risk that controls may become inadequate because of changes in conditions, or that the degree of compliance with policies or procedures may deteriorate.

We did not test compliance with all laws and regulations applicable to the Commission. We limited our tests of compliance to those laws and regulations that have a direct and material effect on the financial statements for the fiscal year ended September 30, 2011. We caution that noncompliance may occur and not be detected by these tests and that such testing may not be sufficient for other purposes.

We performed our audit in accordance with U.S. generally accepted government auditing standards. We believe our audit provides a reasonable basis for our opinions and other conclusions.

Commission Comments

In commenting via e-mail on a draft of this report, the Commission concurred with GAO's findings and conclusions.

Steven J. Sebastian

Steven J. Sebastian
Managing Director
Financial Management and Assurance

February 21, 2012

Management's Discussion and Analysis

AMERICAN BATTLE MONUMENTS COMMISSION
ANNUAL FINANCIAL REPORT
MANAGEMENT'S DISCUSSION AND ANALYSIS (MDA)
FOR THE FISCAL YEAR ENDED SEPTEMBER 30, 2011

Mission

The American Battle Monuments Commission (the Commission)   guardian of America's overseas commemorative cemeteries and memorials   honors the service, achievements and sacrifice of the United States armed forces. Since 1923, the Commission has executed this mission by (1) commemorating the achievements and sacrifices of America's armed forces through the erection and maintenance of suitable memorial shrines in the U.S. when authorized by Congress and where they have served overseas since April 6, 1917; (2) designing, constructing, operating, and maintaining permanent American military burial grounds in foreign countries; and (3) controlling the design and construction on foreign soil of U.S. military memorials, monuments, and markers by other U.S. citizens and organizations, both public and private, and encouraging their maintenance. The Commission's fiscal year 2011 appropriation supported its continued commitment to the worldwide responsibilities that flow from this mission.

In performance of its mission, the Commission administers, operates, and maintains 24 permanent American military cemeteries; 25 federal memorials, monuments, and markers; and seven nonfederal memorials. Three memorials are located in the United States; the remaining memorials and all of the Commission's cemeteries are located in 14 foreign countries, the U.S. Commonwealth of the Northern Mariana Islands, and the British dependency of Gibraltar. These cemeteries and memorials are among the most beautiful and meticulously maintained shrines in the world. The Commission's World War I, World War II, and Mexico City cemeteries are closed to future burials except for the remains of U.S. war dead discovered in World War I and II battle areas.

In addition to grave sites, the World War I and II cemeteries, together with three memorials on U.S. soil, commemorate by name on Tablets of the Missing those U.S. service members who were missing in action or lost or buried at sea during the First and Second World Wars and the Korean and Vietnam Wars.

The Commission also administers trust funds to (1) build memorials authorized by Congress, but financed primarily from private contributions, commemorative coin proceeds, and investment earnings; (2) decorate grave sites with flowers from private contributions; and (3) maintain and repair nonfederal war memorials with private contributions.

During fiscal year 2011, the Commission continued to ensure that its commemorative cemeteries and memorials remain fitting shrines to those who have served our nation in uniform since America's entry into World War I.

1

The Commission's mission statement:

> *The American Battle Monuments Commission — guardian of America's overseas commemorative cemeteries and memorials — honors the competence, courage, and sacrifice of United States armed forces.*

Organizational Structure

The Commission's organizational structure for fiscal year 2011 is shown in figure 1.

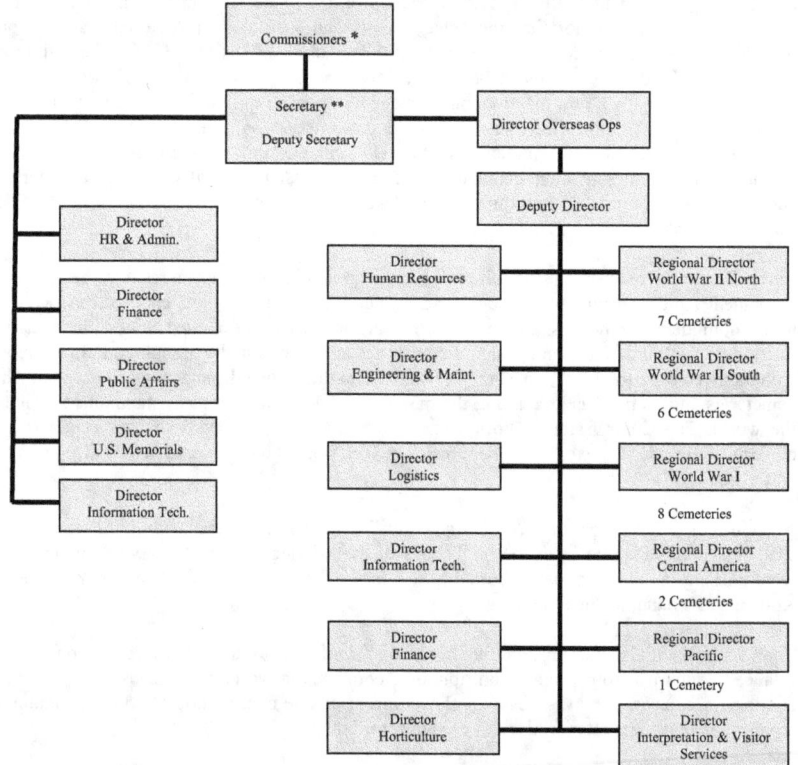

* Chairman and up to 10 Commissioners appointed by the President

** Appointed by the President

Figure 1: The Commission's Organizational Structure

2

The Commission's policy making body consists of an 11 member Board of Commissioners appointed by the President of the United States for an indefinite term and whose members serve without pay. However, the members of the Commission may receive reimbursement for actual expenses related to the work and travel of the Commission. The commissioners establish policy and ensure proper staff functioning in carrying out the mission of the Commission. During inspection visits to Commission cemeteries, they observe, inquire about, comment upon, and make recommendations on any and all aspects of Commission operations. The Commission's daily operations are directed by an Executive Level Secretary, who is appointed by the President and assisted by a Deputy Secretary.

The Commission's headquarters is in Arlington, Virginia and an Office of Overseas Operations is located in Garches, France, just outside Paris. For fiscal year 2011, the Commission had a total of 396 full time equivalent (FTE) positions.

Operations Management

Operations management activities in fiscal year 2011 focused on funding salaries and benefits, service fees, scheduled maintenance and repairs, supplies, materials, spare parts, replacement of uneconomically repairable equipment, and capital improvements.

For fiscal year 2011, the Commission received $64,071,600 from appropriations in its Salaries and Expenses account. The Commission's Foreign Currency Fluctuations Account appropriation for fiscal year 2011 contained "such sums as may be necessary" language. For fiscal year 2011, the Commission estimated $15,968,000 be used to offset currency exchange losses. Figure 2 shows how the Commission obligated funding from its Salaries and Expenses account, by object class.

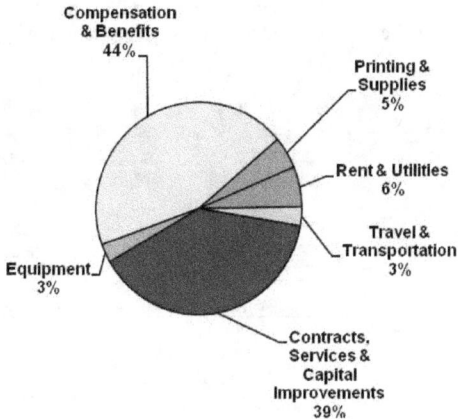

Figure 2: Fiscal Year 2011 Obligations by Object Class

3

The Commission has received funding for engineering, maintenance and horticulture programs that make the Commission's facilities among the most beautiful memorials in the world. These shrines to America's war dead require a formidable annual program of maintenance and repair of facilities, equipment, and grounds.

The Commission prioritizes the use of its engineering, maintenance and horticulture funds carefully to ensure the most effective and efficient utilization of its available resources. This care includes upkeep of more than 131,000 graves and headstones and 73 memorial structures (within and external to the cemeteries) on approximately 1,650 acres of land. Additionally, the Commission maintains 65 visitor facilities and quarters for assigned personnel; 67 miles of roads and paths; 911 acres of flowering plants, fine lawns, and meadows; 3 million square feet of shrubs and hedges; and 11,000 ornamental trees.

Care and maintenance of these resources requires exceptionally intensive labor at the Commission's cemeteries and memorials. Compensation and benefits consumed approximately 44 percent of the Commission's fiscal year 2011 spending while the remaining 56 percent supported engineering, maintenance, horticulture, logistics, services, supplies and other administrative costs critical to its operations.

Financial Analysis

Assets

The Consolidated Balance Sheet reflects total assets of $82.9 million at the end of FY 2011, an increase of $8.5 million over the $74.4 million at the end of FY 2010. The Fund Balance with Treasury and Treasury Investment line items increased by $9 million, as construction projects had been obligated by fiscal year end, but payments had not yet commenced. Total assets are comprised of $72.2 million in the General Fund and $10.7 million in the Trust Fund. The Commission's assets reflected in the Consolidated Balance Sheet are as follows:

ASSETS BY TYPE

Dollars in Thousands	2011	%	2010	%
Fund Balance with Treasury	75,990,111	92%	62,424,270	84%
Investments, Net	4,531,154	5%	9,077,064	12%
Cash and Foreign Accounts	139,225	0%	163,540	0%
Accounts Receivable and Employee Advances	6,751	0%	4,747	0%
General Property and Equipment, Net	2,278,459	3%	2,775,546	4%
Total Assets	82,945,700	100%	74,445,167	100%

4

Liabilities

The Commission's Consolidated Balance Sheet reflects total liabilities of $9 million at the end of FY 2011, which represents a slight increase from the previous year's total liabilities of $8.6 million. Liabilities are categorized as Intragovernmental liabilities or liabilities held with the public. Intragovernmental liabilities totaled $1.8 million in fiscal year 2011 compared to $0.5 million in fiscal year 2010. The increase is mainly attributable to the outsourcing of the new financial management system to the Department of Interior   National Business Center. Liabilities held with the public totaled $7.2 million in fiscal year 2011 compared to $8 million in fiscal year 2010. The composition of the Commission's liabilities is as follows:

LIABILITIES BY TYPE

Dollars in Thousands	2011	%	2010	%
Accounts Payable	5,319,786	59%	3,847,000	45%
Accrued Salaries and Benefits	348,853	4%	386,666	4%
Other Liabilities	3,341,304	37%	4,368,135	51%
Total Liabilities	9,009,943	100%	8,601,801	100%

Net Position

The Commission's Consolidated Balance Sheet and Consolidated Statement of Changes in Net Position reflect a Net Position of $73.9 million at the end of FY 2011, a 12 percent increase from the $65.8 million net position in fiscal year 2010. The increase is mainly attributable to the increase in Fund Balance with Treasury. Net Position is the sum of Unexpended Appropriations and Cumulative Results of Operations.

Net Costs

The Commission's total net cost of operations for FY 2011 was $73.5 million. This represents an increase of $3.2 million of the Commission's net cost of operations of $70.3 million in fiscal year 2010. The increase is mainly attributable to the cost associated with the implementation of a new financial management system, increase in engineering, maintenance and horticulture projects, and a general increase in foreign currency losses. Net costs are summarized in the table below.

NET COSTS

Dollars in Thousands	2011	%	2010	%
Operations and Maintenance	58,626,668	80%	52,783,781	75%
Property and Equipment	2,180,338	7%	6,482,130	9%
Foreign Currency Losses, Net	12,697,365	17%	11,032,311	16%
Net Costs of Operations	73,504,371	100%	70,298,222	100%

5

Budgetary Resources

The Consolidated Statement of Budgetary Resources provides information on how budgetary resources were made available to the Commission for the year and the status of these resources at fiscal year end. For the 2011 fiscal year, the Commission had total budgetary resources of $127.8 million, which represents a 4% increase from FY 2010 levels of $122.7 million. Budget Authority of $96.2 million consisted of $80.2 million in appropriations received, $15.5 million in appropriations transferred in for net foreign exchange loss, and $0.5 million in other receipts. The Commission incurred obligations totaling $78.0 million in fiscal year 2011 compared with FY 2010 obligations incurred of $75.3 million.

Net Outlays reflect the actual cash disbursed against previously established obligations. For FY 2011, the Commission had net outlays of $71.3 million, compared to $68.6 million in net outlays in fiscal year 2010, an increase of 4 percent.

Heritage Assets

Heritage assets are property, plant and equipment that are unique for one or more of the following reasons: historical or natural significance; cultural, educational, or artistic importance; or significant architectural characteristics.

Heritage assets are significant to the mission of the Commission to design, construct, and maintain historical cemeteries and memorials. The Commission presents its heritage assets in three categories; cemeteries, federal memorials, and nonfederal memorials. Through September 30, 2011, the Commission had 24 cemeteries, 25 federal memorials and 7 nonfederal memorials. Presently, over 131,000 U.S. war dead are interred in these cemeteries. Commemorated individually by name on stone tablets at the cemeteries and federal memorials are over 94,000 Honored War Dead, whose remains were not recovered. The cemeteries and federal memorials encompass over 1,600 acres. This land is provided to the Commission through host nation agreements for permanent use as cemeteries and memorials.

High Priority Performance Goals and Results

Summarized below are the Commission's performance goals and results.

Goal 1: Provide an inspirational and educational visitor experience through effective outreach and interpretive programs.

Objectives for Goal 1

- Educate the public about the ABMC mission, and the competence, courage, and sacrifice of those honored at ABMC commemorative sites.
- Increase visitation to ABMC cemeteries, memorials, and website.
- Educate and train all employees who provide visitor services in interpretive skills.
- Leverage international events and relevant anniversary dates to interpret ABMC cemeteries.
- Satisfy constituents' needs through timely distribution of information and products.

6

Strategy for Achieving Goal 1

We will develop educational materials and new technology capabilities to improve visitor education programs, both on site and on our website. We will expand Web marketing and public/media outreach to increase visitation to our website and memorial sites. We will also develop a methodology to count visitors so that we can document both on site and website visitation. We will expand training and mentoring opportunities to enhance professional and personal development of our employees. We will also create historical reference libraries to assist in the interpretive mission. We will leverage upcoming milestones to increase the public reach of the interpretive initiative, including D Day, Memorial Day, Veterans Day, the 100th anniversary of World War I, the 70th anniversary of World War II, and the 2012 London Olympics. We will automate frequently requested services for our constituents in order to improve on site and website customer service.

Selected Performance Results toward Achieving Goal 1

- A contract was awarded to produce 18 educational military campaign interactive programs for the agency website and visitor centers. The interactive programs will be comparable in scope and content to the "Normandy Campaign" and "Battle of Pointe du Hoc" interactives available now at www.abmc.gov.

- Military units, veterans groups, and local citizens and organizations continued to pay tribute to those honored at ABMC cemeteries by visiting individually or participating in ceremonies and popular "adopt a grave" programs in several European nations.

- Interpretive specialists in the Commission's Overseas Operations Office in France continued a program to train cemetery based staffs on interpretive techniques and effective visitor services programs. Professional reference libraries comprised of general military history as well as books relevant to the wars and campaigns associated with individual cemeteries were completed and continue to be updated to enhance our staffs' ability to interpret historical events for visitors.

- Public outreach to the travel and tourism industry was reenergized in fiscal year 2011 through attendance at several trade shows, conventions, and symposia, generating interest in the Commission's commemorative sites as inspirational and educational tourism destinations.

- New visitor brochures were designed, printed or begun for the final 11 cemeteries requiring them, and an initiative was launched to produce similar brochures for several of the Commission's memorials and monuments worldwide. This program is expected to be completed by the end of fiscal year 2012, at which time the Commission will begin a redesign and rewrite of its cemetery booklets. ABMC continued to respond to customer requests for lithographs, no fee passport authorizations, flower placements, and general information about the overseas cemeteries and memorials we administer.

7

Goal 2: Develop, operate, maintain, and improve ABMC facilities as the world's best commemorative sites.

Objective for Goal 2

- Review and evaluate facilities and execute approved maintenance, repair, and improvements.

Strategy for Achieving Goal 2

We will continue to operate, maintain, and improve ABMC facilities and infrastructure in like new condition, and implement our evaluation processes to ensure compliance with our high standards. We will work to reduce the growth of operational and routine maintenance costs and promote more effective long term planning, operations, and resource management.

Selected Performance Results toward Achieving Goal 2

- The following are examples of the engineering, maintenance and horticulture projects executed in fiscal year 2011:

    Renovate the perimeter road at Sicily Rome American Cemetery
    Repair the storm drainage system at Luxembourg American Cemetery
    Renovate the irrigation system at Manila American Cemetery
    Repair and re level the porphyry stones and travertine slabs near the memorial at Sicily Rome American Cemetery
    Repair the exterior cracked wall near the visitor building at Oise Aisne American Cemetery

- The Commission continued a headstone refurbishing program to keep the headstones in "like new" condition.

Goal 3: Attract and retain quality employees through personal and professional investment and development.

Objectives for Goal 3

- Establish baseline employee satisfaction through an ABMC employee survey.
- Ensure timely and effective employee recognition.
- Implement an enhanced performance management program with annual performance work plans tied to the strategic plan.
- Balance employee personal and professional responsibilities through work/life initiatives.
- Implement a professional development program responsive to agency and employee needs.

8

Strategy for Achieving Goal 3

We will implement a professional training and development program, clearly map employee roles and responsibilities to the components of our strategic plan, develop a better understanding of employee needs and satisfaction, and make sure that truly outstanding performance is appropriately recognized.

Selected Performance Results toward Achieving Goal 3

- ABMC was able to recognize employees in a timely manner in response to special acts over the last year.

- Final drafts of a telework policy and new performance appraisal program were nearing publication as the fiscal year ended.

- Human resource hires from 2010 made progress in developing needed HR policies and streamlining/establishing procedures required for the proper functioning of a good HR program. Among the policies developed and issued were foreign language requirements, a voluntary leave transfer program, flexible work schedules for the Headquarters, a category rating policy, and a position management policy.

- The Commission continues to make progress in providing management and supervisory training to its most visible and important positions   its cemetery superintendents.

Goal 4: Continually improve business and resource management practices.

Objectives for Goal 4

- Effectively manage resources.
- Modernize business processes to utilize new technologies and IT practices.
- Formalize processes for development and promulgation of policies and procedures.
- Modernize the Financial Management System and fully utilize the capabilities of the new system.

Strategy for Achieving Goal 4

We will focus our efforts on standardizing core processes, identifying opportunities to use technology to streamline their execution, improving our organizational standards for site evaluation, and regularly reviewing each site for compliance with standards.

Selected Performance Results toward Achieving Goal 4

- The Commission's allocation processes and procedures annually fully fund its mandatory and operational requirements in order to achieve its mission requirements.

- During fiscal year 2011, the Commission completed an effort to implement a new financial management system.

9

- An internal control review and risk assessment was conducted in fiscal year 2011 to examine the Commission's internal control mechanisms and business processes.

- The Commission continues to report that its internal control policies and procedures provide reasonable assurance that it complies with the provisions of 31 U.S.C. 3512 (c), (d)   Federal Managers' Financial Integrity Act (FMFIA).

Financial Statements and Limitations

Since fiscal year 1997, the Commission has been required to produce financial statements and the Comptroller General of the United States has been required to independently audit these statements. The Commission earned unqualified opinions, each year, on its financial statements from the U.S. Government Accountability Office.

The financial statements have been prepared to report the financial position and results of operations of the Commission, pursuant to the requirements of 31 U.S.C. 3515 (b). While the statements have been prepared from the books and records of the Commission in accordance with generally accepted accounting principles for federal entities and the formats prescribed by the Office of Management and Budget, the statements are in addition to the financial reports used to monitor and control budgetary resources, which are prepared from the same books and records. The statements should be read with the understanding that the Commission is a component of the U.S. Government, a sovereign entity.

Management Integrity: Systems, Controls, Legal Compliance

The Commission is cognizant of the importance of, and need for, management accountability and responsibility as the basis for quality and timeliness of program performance, mission accomplishment, productivity, cost effectiveness, and compliance with applicable laws. It has taken management actions to ensure that the annual evaluation of these controls is performed in a conscientious and thorough manner according to Office of Management and Budget regulations and guidelines and in compliance with 31 U.S.C. 3512 (c), (d), commonly known as the Federal Manager's Financial Integrity Act (FMFIA). The objectives of the Commission's internal management control policies and procedures are to provide reasonable assurance that

- obligations and costs are in compliance with applicable law;

- funds, property, and other assets are safeguarded against waste, loss, unauthorized use, and misappropriation;

- revenue and expenditures applicable to agency operations are promptly recorded and accounted for; and

- programs are efficiently and effectively carried out in accordance with applicable laws and management policy.

10

Based on its evaluation, the Commission concluded that there is reasonable assurance that its internal control over the effectiveness and efficiency of operations and compliance with applicable laws and regulations as of September 30, 2011 was operating effectively and revealed no material weaknesses. The reasonable assurance concept recognizes that the cost of internal controls should not exceed the benefits expected to be derived and that the benefits reduce the risk of failing to achieve stated objectives.

The Commission is also responsible for establishing and maintaining effective internal control over financial reporting. Commission management evaluated the effectiveness of its internal control over financial reporting as of September 30, 2011, based on the criteria established under FMFIA. Based on that evaluation, the Commission concluded that, as of September 30, 2011, internal control over financial reporting was effective.

Future Effects, Risks, and Uncertainties

Changes in the rate of exchange for foreign currencies have a significant impact on the Commission's day to day operations. In order to insulate the Commission's annual appropriation against major changes in its purchasing power, legislation was enacted in 1988 (codified in 36 U.S.C. 2109) to establish a foreign currency fluctuation account in the U.S. Treasury. However, since the summer of 2006, the U.S. dollar has fallen precipitously against the euro. The Commission has been closely monitoring this because its budget is disproportionately affected by foreign currency fluctuation. Legislation was enacted which included "such sums as may be necessary" language for the Commission's fiscal year 2011 Foreign Currency Fluctuation Account (FCFA) appropriation. This allows the Commission to preserve its purchasing power against a suddenly falling U.S. dollar against the euro. With this language the Commission will continue to estimate and report its FCFA requirements as it has in the past. However, when a need arises where the amount forecast by the Commission for this account is insufficient, the Commission will submit an adjusted estimate to the Office of Management and Budget and then, to the Congress.

Overall, by maintaining close scrutiny of the Commission's obligation status, as well as monitoring and distributing the Foreign Currency Fluctuation Account balance, the Commission reduces its overall future financial risk to continued operations.

11

Financial Statements

Consolidating Balance Sheet

AMERICAN BATTLE MONUMENTS COMMISSION
CONSOLIDATING BALANCE SHEET
As of September 30, 2011
(With Comparative Consolidated Total as of September 30, 2010)

	General Fund	Trust Funds	Total Funds	Total Funds
	Cemeteries and Memorials	WWII and Other Trust Funds	Total 2011	Total 2010
Assets				
Intragovernmental:				
Fund balance with Treasury (note 2)	$69,798,270	$6,191,841	$75,990,111	$62,424,270
Treasury investments, net (note 3)		4,531,154	4,531,154	9,077,064
Total Intragovernmental	69,798,270	10,722,995	80,521,265	71,501,334
Cash and foreign accounts (note 4)	139,225		139,225	163,540
Accounts receivable	4,747		4,747	4,747
Employee advances	2,004		2,004	
Contributions receivable, net (note 5)				
General property and equipment, net (note 6)	2,278,459		2,278,459	2,775,546
Heritage property (note 6)				
Total Assets	$72,222,705	$10,722,995	$82,945,700	$74,445,167
Liabilities				
Intragovernmental:				
Accounts payable	$1,435,663		$1,435,663	$156,065
Accrued salaries and benefits	348,853		348,853	386,666
Total Intragovernmental	1,784,516		1,784,516	542,731
Accounts payable	3,863,752	$20,371	3,884,123	3,690,935
Other liabilities (note 7)	3,341,304		3,341,304	4,368,135
Total Liabilities	8,989,572	20,371	9,009,943	8,601,801
Commitments and contingencies (note 12)				
Net Position (note 9)				
Unexpended appropriations	63,578,453		63,578,453	53,552,402
Cumulative results of operations (deficit)	(345,320)	10,702,624	10,357,304	12,290,964
Total Net Position	63,233,133	10,702,624	73,935,757	65,843,366
Total Liabilities and Net Position	$72,222,705	$10,722,995	$82,945,700	$74,445,167

The accompanying notes are an integral part of these statements.

1

Consolidating Statement of Net Cost and Changes in Net Position

AMERICAN BATTLE MONUMENTS COMMISSION
CONSOLIDATING STATEMENT OF NET COST AND CHANGES IN NET POSITION
For the Year Ended September 30, 2011
(With Comparative Consolidated Total for the Year Ended September 30, 2010)

	General Fund	Trust Funds	Total Funds	Total Funds
	Cemeteries and Memorials	WWII and Other Trust Funds	Total 2011	Total 2010
PROGRAM COSTS				
Intragovernmental program costs:				
Operations and maintenance	$17,022,320	$1,807,468	$18,829,788	$11,200,299
Program costs with the public:				
Operations and maintenance	39,588,001	208,879	39,796,880	41,583,482
Property and equipment (note 6)	2,180,338		2,180,338	6,482,130
Foreign currency losses, net	12,697,365		12,697,365	11,032,311
Net Cost of Operations	$71,488,024	$2,016,347	$73,504,371	$70,298,222
CHANGES IN NET POSITION				
Cumulative Results (Deficit) - Start of Year	$64,530	$12,226,434	$12,290,964	$12,484,799
Budgetary Financing Sources				
Appropriations used	69,914,171		69,914,171	68,590,164
Total Budgetary Financing Sources	69,914,171		69,914,171	68,590,164
Other Financing Sources				
Contributions	33,361	423,941	457,302	439,847
Treasury investment earnings		68,596	68,596	73,444
Imputed financing (note 13)	1,099,708		1,099,708	1,000,932
Gain on disposition of assets	30,934		30,934	
Total Other Financing Sources	1,164,003	492,537	1,656,540	1,514,223
Total Financing Sources	71,078,174	492,537	71,570,711	70,104,387
Less: Net Cost of Operations	71,488,024	2,016,347	73,504,371	70,298,222
Net Increase (Decrease) for the Year	(409,850)	(1,523,810)	(1,933,660)	(193,835)
Cumulative Results (Deficit) - End of Year	(345,320)	10,702,624	10,357,304	12,290,964
Unexpended Appropriations				
Unexpended Appropriations - Start of Year	53,552,402		53,552,402	39,267,566
Appropriations received	80,200,000		80,200,000	82,875,000
Appropriations transferred out	(190,187)		(190,187)	
Other offsetting receipts and adjustments	(69,591)		(69,591)	
Appropriations used	(69,914,171)		(69,914,171)	(68,590,164)
Increase (decrease) in unexpended appropriations	10,026,051		10,026,051	14,284,836
Unexpended Appropriations - End of Year	63,578,453		63,578,453	53,552,402
TOTAL NET POSITION - END OF YEAR	$63,233,133	$10,702,624	$73,935,757	$65,843,366

The accompanying notes are an integral part of these statements.

2

Consolidating Statement of Budgetary Resources

AMERICAN BATTLE MONUMENTS COMMISSION
CONSOLIDATING STATEMENT OF BUDGETARY RESOURCES
For the Year Ended September 30, 2011
(With Comparative Consolidated Total for the Year Ended September 30, 2010)

	General Fund	Trust Funds	Total Funds	Total Funds
	Cemeteries and Memorials	WWII and Other Trust Funds	Total 2011	Total 2010
Budgetary Resources				
Budgetary Authority				
Appropriations	$80,200,000		$80,200,000	$82,875,000
Net transfer in for net foreign exchange loss	15,461,665		15,461,665	11,590,892
Other receipts collected		492,536	492,536	530,897
Unobligated Balances				
Start of year	36,121,225	11,228,004	47,349,229	39,276,237
Net transfer (out) for net foreign exchange (loss)	(15,461,665)		(15,461,665)	(11,590,892)
Rescission	(160,400)		(160,400)	
Other adjustments	(42,459)		(42,459)	(27,368)
Total Budgetary Resources	$116,118,366	$11,720,540	$127,838,906	$122,654,766
Status of Budgetary Resources				
Obligations incurred direct (note 14)	76,717,678	1,311,036	$78,028,714	$75,305,537
Unobligated balances available	39 400 688	10 409 504	49 810 193	47 349 229
Total Status of Budgetary Resources	$116,118,366	$11,720,540	$127,838,906	$122,654,766
Change in Obligated Balances				
Obligations incurred for year	$76,717,678	$1,311,036	$78,028,714	$75,305,537
Plus Obligated balances, start of year	23,315,904	1,004,489	24,320,393	17,629,014
Less Gross outlays for year	(69,368,783)	(2,002,034)	(71,370,817)	(68,614,158)
Obligated Balances, End of Year	$30,664,799	$313,491	$30,978,290	$24,320,393
Net Outlays				
Gross outlays for year	69,368,783	$2,002,034	$71,370,817	$68,614,158
Less Offsetting collections	(52,622)		(52,622)	(43,166)
Net Outlays	$69,316,161	$2,002,034	$71,318,195	$68,570,992

The accompanying notes are an integral part of these statements

3

Notes to Consolidating and Consolidated Financial Statements

AMERICAN BATTLE MONUMENTS COMMISSION

NOTES TO CONSOLIDATING AND CONSOLIDATED FINANCIAL STATEMENTS

For the Fiscal Years Ended September 30, 2011 and 2010

Note 1. Significant Accounting Policies

A. Basis of Presentation

The accompanying consolidating and consolidated financial statements present the financial position, net cost of operations, changes in net position, and budgetary resources of the American Battle Monuments Commission (the Commission) in conformity with U.S. generally accepted accounting principles as used by the federal government. There are no intra entity transactions to be eliminated. Certain assets, liabilities, and costs have been classified as intragovernmental throughout the financial statements and notes. Intragovernmental is defined as transactions made between two reporting entities within the federal government.

B. Reporting Entity and Funding Sources

The Commission is an independent agency within the executive branch of the federal government and was created by an Act of March 4, 1923, the current provisions of which are now codified in 36 U.S.C. Chapter 21. The Commission's mission is to commemorate the sacrifices and achievements of U.S. Armed Forces where they have served overseas since April 6, 1917, the date of the United States entry into World War I, and at locations within the United States when directed by the Congress. The Commission designs, administers, constructs, operates, and maintains 24 American military cemeteries and 25 federal memorials, monuments, and markers (herein collectively referred to as memorials). Three of the memorials are located in the United States while all of the cemeteries and the remaining memorials are located on foreign soil in 14 foreign countries, the Marianas, and Gibraltar. The Commission is also responsible for maintaining 7 nonfederal memorials with funds received from the memorials' sponsors. The Commission is headquartered in Arlington, Virginia. Field operations are conducted through offices located near Paris, France and Rome, Italy; and cemeteries in Manila, the Philippines; Mexico City, Mexico; and Panama City, Panama.

The Commission also had responsibility for designing and constructing the National World War II Memorial located on the Mall in Washington, D.C. In accordance with 40 U.S.C. 8906(b), the Commission deposited $6.6 million into a separate Treasury account to offset the memorial's costs of perpetual maintenance. On November 1, 2004, the Commission signed an agreement with the National Park Service to formally transfer the National World War II Memorial to the Service for its future care and maintenance. Remaining funds reside in a trust fund in the U.S. Treasury to be used solely to benefit the World War II Memorial for other than routine maintenance expense.

Commission programs are funded primarily through appropriations available without fiscal year limitation (no year). The Commission also administers several trust funds established to: (1) build memorials authorized by the Congress, but which are funded primarily by private contributions, commemorative coin sales proceeds, and investment earnings; (2) decorate gravesites; and (3) maintain and repair certain nonfederal war memorials.

4

C. Basis of Accounting

The Commission's proprietary accounts (assets, liabilities, equity, revenue, and expenses) are maintained on the accrual basis, where appropriated funds are accounted for by appropriation year; operating expenses are recorded as incurred; and depreciation is taken on property, plant, and equipment not otherwise classified as heritage assets. Commission budgetary accounts are maintained on a budgetary basis, which facilitates compliance with legal constraints and statutory funds control requirements. The functional budget classification is Veterans' Benefits and Services.

D. Fund Balances with Treasury

The Commission's cash receipts and disbursements are processed by the U.S. Treasury. Fund balances with Treasury are composed of appropriated general funds and trust funds. The Fund balance with Treasury is the aggregate amount for which the Commission is authorized to make expenditures and pay liabilities.

E. Investments

In accordance with 36 U.S.C. 2113(b), the Commission is authorized to invest World War II Memorial Trust Fund receipts in U.S. Treasury securities. The Commission is also authorized under a modification to its original legislation to invest receipts from certain nonfederal war memorial organizations in U.S. Treasury securities. Treasury investments are recorded at par value plus unamortized premium or less unamortized discount. Premiums and discounts are amortized using the interest method.

F. Foreign Currency

The Commission's overseas offices maintain accounts of foreign currencies to be used in making payments in foreign countries. Amounts are recorded at a standard budget rate in U.S. dollars and a gain or loss recognized when paid in foreign currency. Appropriated monies are transferred from the Commission's Foreign Currency Fluctuation Account to fund net currency losses. Cash accounts in foreign currencies are reported at the U.S. dollar equivalent using the Treasury exchange rate in effect on the last day of the fiscal year.

G. Contributions and Revenue Recognition

The Commission recognizes unrestricted contributions or unconditional promises to give as revenue in the period of the initial pledge when sufficient verifiable evidence of the pledge exists. Conditional promises to give are recorded as revenue when the condition has been met. Unconditional promises to give may be temporarily restricted or permanently restricted. Temporarily restricted promises to give are released from restriction when the conditions have been met. Permanently restricted promises to give are recorded as revenue in the period donated; however, donors generally allow only the earned income to be used for general or specific purposes. In kind contributions of goods and services are recognized at fair value by the Commission at the time the goods are received or the services are performed. Multiyear contributions due over a period of time are discounted to their present value based upon the short term Treasury interest rate.

5

H. Operating Materials and Supplies Inventories

The Commission has determined that operating materials and supplies located at its cemeteries are not significant amounts and that it is more cost beneficial to record them on the purchase method of accounting whereby items are expensed as purchased rather than when consumed. Consequently, the Commission reports no operating materials or supplies inventories.

I. Property and Equipment

Purchases of general property and equipment of $25,000 or less are expensed in the year of acquisition. Purchases of personal property exceeding $25,000 are capitalized and depreciated on a straight line basis over 5 years. Expenditures relating to real property exceeding $25,000 are capitalized and depreciated on a straight line basis over 30 years. Heritage assets are assets possessing significant cultural, architectural, or aesthetic characteristics. The Commission considers its cemeteries, and federal memorials, monuments, and markers acquired through purchase or donation to be noncollection heritage assets. Heritage assets acquired through purchase or donation are accounted for in the Commission's property records, and are not presented in the balance sheet. Withdrawals of heritage assets are recorded upon formal agreement with recipients. Additional disclosure on individual heritage asset cemeteries and memorials are found in the Schedules of Heritage Assets presented as unaudited other information. Cemetery land is owned by the foreign countries in which cemeteries are located and is provided to the United States in perpetuity.

J. Employee Benefits

The Commission's civilian U.S. nationals hired after December 31, 1983 are covered by the Federal Employees' Retirement System (FERS), which was implemented on January 1, 1984. The Commission's civilian U.S. nationals hired on or before December 31, 1983, could elect to transfer to FERS or remain with the Civil Service Retirement System (CSRS). For FERS employees, the Commission withholds .80 percent of base pay and as employer contributes 11.7 percent of base pay to this retirement system. For Federal Insurance Contribution Act (FICA) tax and Medicare, the Commission withholds 5.65 percent from FERS employees' earnings. In addition, the Commission contributes 7.65 percent and remits the total amount to the Social Security Administration. The Commission withholds 7.00 percent of base pay plus 1.45 percent for Medicare from CSRS employees' earnings and as employer contributes 7.00 percent of base pay plus 1.45 percent for Medicare. These deductions are then remitted to the Office of Personnel Management (OPM) and the Social Security Administration. OPM is responsible for governmentwide reporting of FERS and CSRS assets, accumulated plan benefits, and unfunded liabilities.

On April 1, 1987, the federal government instituted the Thrift Saving Plan (TSP), a retirement savings and investment plan for employees covered by FERS and CSRS. The Commission contributes a minimum of 1 percent of FERS employees' base pay to TSP. For 2011, FERS employees could contribute up to $16,500 ($22,000 if at least age 50) on a tax deferred basis to TSP, which the Commission matches up to 4 percent of base pay. For 2011, CSRS employees may also contribute up to $16,500 ($22,000 if at least age 50) on a tax deferred basis; however, they receive no matching contribution from the Commission.

6

Retirement and other benefits for the Commission's foreign national employees are paid by the Commission in accordance with the provisions of 10 host nation agreements negotiated by the U.S. Department of State.

Annual leave is accrued as earned, and the resulting unfunded liability is reduced as leave is taken. Separation pay is provided in certain countries according to host nation agreements. Separation pay is accrued as earned, and the resulting unfunded liability is reduced when paid to the foreign national leaving the employ of the Commission. Each year balances in the accrued separation pay and annual leave accounts are adjusted to reflect current pay rates. To the extent that current or prior year appropriations are not available to fund annual leave and separation pay, funding will be obtained from future financing resources. Sick leave and other types of unvested leave are expensed when incurred.

K. Program Costs

Program costs are broken out into two categories "Intragovernmental" and "With the Public". Intragovernmental costs are costs the Commission incurs through contracting with other federal agencies for goods and/or services, such as rent paid to U.S. Department of State, payroll processing services received from the U.S. General Services Administration (GSA), and costs for retirement and other benefits paid by OPM. With the Public costs are costs the Commission incurs through contracting with the private sector for goods or services, payments for employee salaries, depreciation, annual leave and other non Federal entity expenses.

L. Use of Estimates

The preparation of financial statements requires management to make estimates and assumptions that affect the reported amount of assets and liabilities, as well as the disclosure of contingent assets and liabilities at the date of the financial statements, and the amount of revenues and expenses reported during the reporting period. Actual results could differ from those estimates.

7

Note 2. Fund Balances with Treasury

All undisbursed account balances with the U.S. Treasury, as reflected in the Commission's records, as of September 30 are available and were as follows:

	2011			2010
	General Fund	Trust Funds	Total	Total
Appropriated Funds	$46,440,675		$46,440,675	$36,227,394
Currency Fluctuation	23,357,595		23,357,595	23,041,447
Other Trust Funds		$6,191,841	6,191,841	3,155,429
	$69,798,270	$6,191,841	$75,990,111	$62,424,270

Note 3. Treasury Investments, Net

As of September 30, the Commission's Trust Fund investments in U.S. Treasury notes, which are marketable securities due within 2 years were as follows:

		Interest			
FY	Cost	Interest Rates	Net Premium	Interest Receivables	Net Investments
11	$4 368 932	4 250 to 4 50%	$162 222	$0	$4 531 154
10	$8,834,026	4.250 to 5.0%	$156,464	$86,574	$9,077,064

Amortization is on the interest method, with amortized cost approximated to market as of September 30.

Note 4. Cash and Foreign Accounts

Outside the United States, the Commission makes payments in U.S. and foreign currencies through imprest cash funds and Treasury designated depository commercial bank accounts, which as of September 30 were as follows:

	2011	2010
Imprest Cash Funds	$2,284	$40,636
Foreign Bank Accounts	136,941	122,142
Undeposited Cash Trust	0	763
	$139,225	$163,540

Note 5. Contributions Receivable

The Commission has a pledge from a living trust valued at $125,819 as of September 30, 2011. However, due to the uncertainty of time and amount when the pledge is collected, the contribution will be recognized when received.

8

Note 6. General and Heritage Property and Equipment

Non capitalized assets, such as general property and equipment acquisitions with an aggregate cost basis of $25,000 or less and all acquisitions of heritage assets, totaling $2,180,338, were expensed by the Commission in fiscal year 2011. In fiscal year 2010, $6,482,130 was expensed.

Since the 1960s, the Commission's Office of Overseas Operations near Paris, France, has occupied a residential structure owned by the United States government. The Commission is responsible for all utilities, maintenance, and repairs. While the structure has the characteristics of a heritage asset, it has been used as general property. However, it is now fully depreciated, and no value is contained in the Commission's financial statements.

General property and equipment as of September 30 was as follows:

Category	2011			2010		
	Cost	Accumulated Depreciation	Net	Cost	Accumulated Depreciation	Net
Buildings	$923,460	$225,507	$697,953	$923,460	$196,068	$727,392
Accounting Systems	384,951	242,179	142,772	2,145,016	1,929,838	215,178
Equipment	4,372,562	2,934,828	1,437,734	4,522,998	2,690,022	1,832,976
	$5,680,973	$3,402,514	$2,278,459	$7,591,474	$4,815,928	$2,775,546

Heritage assets are significant to the mission of the Commission to design, construct, and maintain historical cemeteries and memorials. The Commission presents its heritage assets in three categories; cemeteries, federal memorials, and nonfederal memorials. Changes in heritage assets for fiscal year 2011 were as follows:

	Cemeteries	Federal Memorials	Nonfederal Memorials
Beginning of Year 10 1 10	24	25	7
Number Acquired, Fiscal Year 2011	0	0	0
Number Withdrawn, Fiscal Year 2011	0	0	0
End of Year 9 30 11	24	25	7

Through September 30, 2011, Commission cemeteries contain over 131,000 interments. Over 94,000 Honored War Dead, whose remains were not recovered, are memorialized in the cemeteries and federal memorials that encompass over 1,600 acres. This land is provided to the Commission through host agreements with foreign countries for permanent use as cemeteries and memorials.

9

Note 7. Other Liabilities

Other liabilities as of September 30 were as follows:

	2011	2010
Accrued Salaries and Benefits	$717,551	$1,657,119
Unfunded Separation Pay Liability	1,212,663	1,393,036
Unfunded Annual Leave	1,411,090	1,317,980
	$3,341,304	$4,368,135

These liabilities are all classified as current.

Under a host nation agreement, the Commission's Italian employees earn separation pay for each year of service with the Commission. The Commission recognized an unfunded liability for separation pay for these employees of $1,212,663 as of September 30, 2011, and $1,393,036 as of September 30, 2010.

Note 8. Lease Agreements

The Commission has no capital leases. The Commission's Arlington, Virginia, Headquarters Office is rented under a 5 year operating lease expiring in July 2012. Future minimum payments due on this operating lease as of September 30, 2011, are as follows:

Fiscal Year	
2012	$570,932
2013	0
2014	0
2015	0
2016	0
After 5 Years	$570,932

The Commission's Rome Office moved from commercial leased space to the United States Embassy in Rome. Lease payments for the Rome office space, and for nine living quarters leases for the benefit of the Commission's Office of Overseas Operations, are made through the International Cooperative Administrative Support Services (ICASS) program with the U.S. State Department. These leases are on a month to month basis and the Commission has no obligation for future payments associated with these leases.

Rent expense for all operating leases was $829,154 during fiscal year 2011.

10

Note 9. Net Position

Net position balances as of September 30, 2011, were as follows:

	General Fund	Trust Funds	Total
Unexpended Appropriations:			
Unobligated	$39,400,688		$39,400,688
Undelivered Orders	24,177,765		24,177,765
	$63,578,453	$	$63,578,453
Cumulative Results of Operations (deficit):			
Unrestricted	($345,320)	$10,409,505	$10,064,185
Restricted for Undelivered Orders		293,119	293,119
	($345,320)	$10,702,624	$10,357,304
Total Net Position	$63,233,133	$10,702,624	$73,935,757

Net position balances as of September 30, 2010, were as follows:

	General Fund	Trust Funds	Total
Unexpended Appropriations:			
Unobligated	$36,121,225		$36,121,225
Undelivered Orders	17,431,177		17,431,177
	$53,552,402	$	$53,552,402
Cumulative Results of Operations (deficit):			
Unrestricted	$64,530	$11,228,004	$11,292,534
Restricted for Undelivered Orders		998,430	998,430
	$64,530	$12,226,434	$12,290,964
Total Net Position	$53,616,932	$12,226,434	$65,843,366

11

Note 10. Reconciliation of Net Cost of Operations to Budget

SFFAS No. 7 requires a reconciliation of proprietary and budgetary information in a way that helps users determine how budget resources obligated for programs relate to net costs of operations. Prior to fiscal year 2007, this reconciliation was accomplished by presenting a Statement of Financing as a basic financial statement. Effective for fiscal year 2007, the Office of Management and Budget in its Circular No. A 136, *Financial Reporting Requirements*, decided that this information for federal entities would be better placed and understood in a note. Consequently, this information is presented as follows:

	General Fund	Trust Funds	Total Funds	Total Funds
	Cemeteries and Memorials	WWII and Other Trust Funds	Total 2011	Total 2010
Resources Used To Finance Activities				
Obligations incurred direct	$76,717,678	$1,311,036	$78,028,714	$75,305,537
Offsetting collections and recoveries	(52,622)		(52,622)	(43,166)
Imputed retirement and audit services	1,099,708		1,099,708	1,000,932
Other adjustments	35,085		35,085	98,634
Total Resources Used to Finance Activities	77,799,848	1,311,036	79,110,884	76,361,937
Resources That Do Not Fund Net Cost of Operations				
General property capitalized on the balance sheet	(259,876)		(259,876)	(599,582)
Undelivered orders start of year	17,431,177	998,430	18,429,607	12,459,352
Less: Undelivered orders end of year	(24,177,765)	(293,119)	(24,470,884)	(18,429,607)
Total Resources That Do Not Fund Net Cost of Operations	(7,006,464)	705,311	(6,301,153)	(6,569,837)
Components of Net Cost of Operations Not Requiring Resources in the Current Period				
Components Requiring Resources in Future Periods:				
(Decrease) Increase in unfunded annual leave	93,110		93,110	49,661
(Decrease) increase in unfunded separation pay liability	(180,373)		(180,373)	(281,259)
Increase in accounts receivable				4,747
Increase in advances	2,004		2,004	
Components Not Requiring Resources:				
Depreciation	746,538		746,539	707,413
In kind expenses	33,361		33,361	25,560
Total Costs Not Requiring Resources in the Current Period	694,640		694,640	506,122
Total Resources Used to Finance the Net Cost of Operations	$71,488,024	$2,016,347	$73,504,371	$70,298,222

12

Note 11. Fiduciary Activities

Fiduciary activities are the collection or receipt, and the management, protection, accounting, investment and disposition by the Federal Government of cash or other assets in which non Federal individuals or entities have an ownership interest that the Federal Government must uphold.

Fiduciary cash and other assets are not assets of the Federal Government and accordingly are not recognized on the balance sheet.

The Scottish Widows Defined Benefit Scheme was established by a Trust Deed, which authorized the Commission to collect contributions on behalf of beneficiaries, foreign service national employees of the Commission's two cemeteries in England. Fiduciary assets as of September 30 were as follows:

Schedule of Fiduciary Activity

	2011	2010
Contributions	$280,926	$79,791
Investment earnings	49,231	36,827
Increases in fiduciary fund balances	330,157	116,618
Fiduciary net assets, beginning of year	942,151	825,533
Fiduciary net assets, end of year	$1,272,308	$942,151

Fiduciary Net Assets

	2011	2010
Fiduciary Assets		
Investments	$1,272,308	$942,151
Total Fiduciary Assets	$1,272,308	$942,151

Note 12. Commitments and Contingencies

As of September 30, 2011, the Commission had commitments of $24.5 million from undelivered orders as a result of open contracts and purchase orders. Also, the Commission had contingencies related to pending administrative proceedings and personnel actions that will be resolved by future events. The Commission has determined the likelihood of an unfavorable outcome is remote and is not expected to have a material effect on the financial statements.

13

Note 13. Imputed Financing

The Commission imputes financing for retirement and other benefits paid by OPM, financial audit costs incurred by the U.S. Government Accountability Office (GAO), and a heritage asset musical carillon donated each fiscal year. The Commission recognized these expenses and related imputed financing in its financial statements. A heritage asset musical carillon was also recognized for this fiscal year as a donation by AMVETS and an in kind expense.

A portion of pension and other retirement benefits (ORB) expense is funded by an imputed financing source to recognize the amount of pension and ORB unfunded liabilities assumed by OPM. These costs are computed in accordance with cost factors provided by OPM. For fiscal year 2011, the Commission incurred $1,799,724 of pension and ORB costs, $550,708 of which was imputed. For fiscal year 2010, the Commission incurred $1,496,691 of pension and ORB costs, $501,932 of which was imputed. Total imputed costs of $1,099,708 for fiscal year 2011 and $1,000,932 for fiscal year 2010 included audit services provided by GAO.

Note 14. Obligations Incurred

All obligations incurred are characterized as category A on the Statement of Budgetary Resources. Currently, the Commission does not have reimbursable obligations.

Note 15. Budgetary Resource Comparisons to the Budget of the United States Government

Statement of Federal Financial Accounting Standards No. 7, "Accounting for Revenue and Other Financing Sources and Concepts for Reconciling Budgetary and Financial Accounting", calls for explanations of material differences between amounts reported in the Statement of Budgetary Resources and the actual balances published in the Budget of the United States Government (President's Budget). The President's Budget for fiscal year 2013 was published in February 2012 and can be found at the OMB Web site: http://www.whitehouse.gov/omb/. There were no material differences between the amounts reported in the fiscal year 2011 Consolidating Statement of Budgetary Resources and the fiscal year 2011 "Actual" column in the 2013 Budget of the United States Government.

14

Other Information

American Battle Monuments Commission
Other Information
September 30, 2011
(Unaudited)

Maintenance, Repairs, and Improvements

The following unaudited information is required supplementary information on deferred maintenance and the condition of real property at Commission cemeteries and memorials:

Deferred maintenance is maintenance that was not performed when it should have been or was scheduled to be and that, therefore, is put off or delayed for a future period. Maintenance and repairs performed on real property consisting of land improvements, buildings, and memorials totaled $6.8 million in fiscal year 2011 and $10.0 million in fiscal year 2010. For fiscal years 1998 through 2002, the Commission received $11.3 million of additional appropriations from the Congress that enabled it to entirely eliminate its deferred maintenance backlog as of September 30, 2002. No deferred maintenance backlog existed as of September 30, 2011, and 2010.

In addition to condition assessment surveys, the Commission uses a Project Prioritization Methodology with a "plot area out" focus to identify current and future maintenance and repair projects at cemeteries and memorials in order to maintain real property in an acceptable condition. These surveys are reviewed and updated at least annually by the Commission's engineering staff. In addition, engineering projects identified improvements in cemetery irrigation, drainage, roads, parking areas, and buildings. As of September 30, 2011, the Commission has identified 43 maintenance, repair, and improvement projects, with an estimated cost of $7.1 million, scheduled to be performed in fiscal year 2012, subject to available funding.

Schedules of Heritage Assets

The following three pages present unaudited other information not required by U.S. generally accepted accounting principles on the Commission's 24 cemeteries; 25 federal memorials, monuments, and markers; and 7 nonfederal memorials as of September 30, 2011.

15

Schedules of Heritage Assets

American Battle Monuments Commission
Schedule of Heritage Assets
September 30, 2011
(Unaudited)

24 CEMETERIES

Name	Location	Interred	Memorialized	Acres	War
Aisne-Marne American Cemetery	Belleau (Aisne), France	2,289	1,060	42.5	WW I
Ardennes American Cemetery	Neupre, Belgium	5,323	462	90.5	WW II
Brittany American Cemetery	St. James (Manche), France	4,410	498	27.9	WW II
Brookwood American Cemetery	Brookwood, England	468	563	4.5	WW I
Cambridge American Cemetery	Cambridge, England	3,812	5,127	30.5	WW II
Corozal American Cemetery	Panama City, Panama	5,418	0	16.0	*
Epinal American Cemetery	Epinal (Vosges), France	5,255	424	48.6	WW II
Flanders Field American Cemetery	Waregem, Belgium	368	43	6.2	WW I
Florence American Cemetery	Florence, Italy	4,402	1,409	70.0	WW II
Henri-Chapelle American Cemetery	Henri-Chapelle, Belgium	7,992	450	57.0	WW II
Lorraine American Cemetery	St. Avold (Moselle), France	10,489	444	113.5	WW II
Luxembourg American Cemetery	Luxembourg City, Luxembourg	5,076	371	50.5	WW II
Manila American Cemetery	Luzon, Phillippines	17,202	36,285	152.0	WW II
Meuse-Argonne American Cemetery	Romagne (Meuse), France	14,246	954	130.5	WW I
Mexico City National Cemetery	Mexico City, Mexico	1,563	0	1.0	**
Netherlands American Cemetery	Margraten, Holland	8,301	1,722	65.5	WW II
Normandy American Cemetery	Colleville-sur-Mer, France	9,387	1,557	172.5	WW II
North Africa American Cemetery	Carthage, Tunisia	2,841	3,724	27.0	WW II
Oise-Aisne American Cemetery	Fere-en-Tardenois, France	6,012	241	36.5	WW I
Rhone American Cemetery	Draguignan, Var, France	861	294	12.5	WW II
St. Mihiel American Cemetery	Thiaucourt, Meurthe, France	4,153	284	40.5	WW I
Sicily-Rome American Cemetery	Nettuno, Italy	7,861	3,095	77.0	WW II
Somme American Cemetery	Bony (Aisne), France	1,844	333	14.3	WW I
Suresnes American Cemetery	Suresnes, France	1,565	974	7.5	WW I/II
Subtotal for Cemeteries		131,138	60,314	1,294.5	

*Acquired by Executive Order as a result of the Panama Canal Treaty.
**Acquired by Executive Order from the War Department.

16

American Battle Monuments Commission
Schedule of Heritage Assets
September 30, 2011
(Unaudited)

25 FEDERAL MEMORIALS, MONUMENTS, AND MARKERS

Name	Location	Interred	Memorialized	Acres	War
East Coast Memorial	New York City, NY		4,609	0.8	WW II
Honolulu Memorial	Honolulu, HI		28,800	1.0	WW II/Korea/Vietnam
West Coast Memorial	San Francisco, CA		412	1.3	WW II
Audenarde Monument	Audenarde, Belgium			0.4	WW I
Bellicourt Monument	St. Quentin, France			1.8	WW I
Brest Naval Monument	Brest, France			1.0	WW I
Cabanatuan Memorial	Luzon, Phillipines				WW II
Cantigny Monument	Cantigny, France			0.4	WW I
Chateau-Thierry Monument	Chateau-Thierry, France			58.9	WW I
Chaumont Marker	Chaumont, France				WW I
Gibraltar Naval Monument	Gibraltar			0.1	WW I
Guadalcanal Memorial	Guadalcanal			0.5	WW II
Kemmel Monument	Ypres, Belgium			0.2	WW I
Marine Monument Belleau Wood	Aisne, France			199.6	WW I
Montfaucon Monument	Montfaucon, France			9.6	WW I
Montsec Monument	Thiaucourt, France			47.5	WW I
Papua Marker	Port Moresby, New Guinea				WW II
Pointe du Hoc Ranger Monument	St. Laurent-sur-Mer, France			29.8	WW II
Saipan Monument	Saipan, Northern Mariana Islands				WW II
Santiago Surrender Tree	Santiago, Cuba				Sp American War
Sommepy Monument	Sommepy, France			15.0	WW I
Souilly Marker	Souilly, France				WW I
Tours Monument	Tours, France			0.5	WW I
Utah Beach Monument	Sainte Marie-du-Mont, France			0.5	WW II
Western Naval Task Force Marker	Casablanca, Morocco				WW II
Subtotal for Memorials		0	33,821	368.9	
Grand Total		131,138	94,135	1,663.4	

17

American Battle Monuments Commission
Schedule of Heritage Assets
September 30, 2011
(Unaudited)

7 NONFEDERAL MEMORIALS

Name	Location	War
29th Infantry Division Memorial	Vierville sur Mer, France	WW II
30th Infantry Division Memorial	Mortain, France	WW II
6th Engineering Special Brigade Memorial	Vierville sur Mer, France	WW II
351st Bomb Group Memorial	Oundle, England	WW II
147th Engineer Battalion Monument	Englesqueville la Percee, France	WW II
507th Parachute Infantry Regiment Memorial	Amfreville, France	WW II
398th Bomb Group Memorial	Herdfordshire, England	WW II

18

Management's Report on Internal Control over Financial Reporting

AMERICAN BATTLE MONUMENTS COMMISSION
Courthouse Plaza II, Suite 500
2300 Clarendon Boulevard
Arlington, VA 22201-3367

Established by Congress 1923

Mr. Steven J. Sebastian
Director, Financial Management and Assurance
U.S. Government Accountability Office
441 G Street, N.W.
Washington, D.C. 20548

Dear Mr. Sebastian:

The American Battle Monuments Commission's internal control over financial reporting is a process affected by those charged with governance, management, and other personnel, designed to provide reasonable assurance regarding the preparation of reliable financial statements in accordance with U.S. generally accepted accounting principles (GAAP). The Commission's internal control over financial reporting is designed to reasonably assure that (1) transactions are properly recorded, processed, and summarized to permit the preparation of financial statements in accordance with U.S. GAAP, and assets are safeguarded against loss from unauthorized acquisition, use, or disposition; and (2) transactions are executed in accordance with the laws governing the use of budget authority and other laws and regulations that could have a direct and material effect on the financial statements.

Commission management is responsible for establishing and maintaining effective internal control over financial reporting. Commission management evaluated the effectiveness of its internal control over financial reporting as of September 30, 2011, based on the criteria established under 31 U.S.C. 3512 (c), (d) (commonly known as the Federal Manager's Financial Integrity Act). Based on that evaluation, we conclude that, as of September 30, 2011, the Commission's internal control over financial reporting was effective.

Max Cleland
Secretary

Christine Philpot
Chief Financial Officer

February 21, 2012